What People Are S[...]

Too Much and Not Enough

Tamra Satler's book *Too Much and Not Enough: Healing for the Enneagram Four or Borderline-Style Personality* offers a rare look into the inner workings of borderline features, which can appear in any of the nine Enneagram points, and the characteristic worldview of point Four. Tamra takes us along her journey of understanding and recovering from the destructive elements of these two psychological tendencies while also sharing her discovery of the many beautiful and beneficial aspects of these orientations. Beyond this, Tamra provides numerous examples of clients working through their particular borderline issues, as well as tools for growth and transformation—both psychological and spiritual. This book will provide not only hope and inspiration for anyone suffering from these personality features but also insight and suggestions for those of us living and working with such individuals. This is a courageous and powerful offering.

Russ Hudson, author of *The Enneagram: Nine Gateways to Presence* and co-author of *The Wisdom of the Enneagram*.

Tamra Sattler's *Too Much and Not Enough* is a beautiful book about a very particular personality type, the Enneagram 4, or Borderline-style personality. But since Fours experience themselves and life more deeply than others, it is actually a soulful journey into humanity's own plump, loving, tragic, and broken heart. Using emotion-driven personal narrative and scholarly research, Sattler reveals the ecstasy and agony that Fours experience practically daily. In a sense, the Four longs for it all ... *now!* Love, God, sorrow, joy, and every bittersweet feeling in between. Sattler doesn't stop at describing the Four, however. She also presents a path forward so that her readers might find more ease and belonging in a world that doesn't always see them as the gift to humanity that they are. If you are a Four or you have a Four in your life, this book is a must read. **Brad Wetzler,** author and book editor

As a long-time sufferer of Borderline Personality Disorder (BPD), who broke free from the cage and experienced the healing that Dr. Sattler describes, I'll say that this book felt like a reflection from the first page. Dr. Sattler's East-West balanced approach to topics that affect intensely feeling people is insightful and groundbreaking, including her emphasis on the need for a strong sense of self.

"Identity Disturbance" is a trait that troubles many people with BPD (it was the symptom that led to my diagnosis). In this book, Dr. Sattler shines a light on the dialectic that a lack of identity can be challenging in a Western context. However, it can also be a catalyst for deeply discovering our interconnectedness, healthy interdependence with others and, ultimately, our true Self.

As a graduate student in Consciousness and Human Potential, Dr. Sattler's description of the Enneagram as a tool for self-discovery, a unique and powerful lens for understanding BPD traits, and guidance for those who feel intensely is particularly appealing. Anyone interested in these topics will enjoy this book! **Debbie DeMarco Bennett** (aka Debbie Corso), BSc., MA in progress, founder of HealingFromBPD.com and EmotionallySensitive.com

Too Much and Not Enough

Healing for the Enneagram Four or
Borderline-Style Personality

Too Much and Not Enough

Healing for the Enneagram Four or Borderline-Style Personality

Tamra Sattler, PhD

MANTRA
BOOKS

Winchester, UK
Washington, USA

JOHN HUNT PUBLISHING

First published by Mantra Books, 2024
Mantra Books is an imprint of John Hunt Publishing Ltd., No. 3 East Street, Alresford
Hampshire SO24 9EE, UK
office@jhpbooks.com
www.johnhuntpublishing.com
www.mantra-books.net

For distributor details and how to order please visit the 'Ordering' section on our website.

Text copyright: Tamra Sattler, PhD 2023

ISBN: 978 1 80341 549 9
978 1 80341 557 4 (ebook)
Library of Congress Control Number: 2023936430

A CIP catalogue record for this book is available from the British Library.

Design: Lapiz Digital Services

UK: Printed and bound by CPI Group (UK) Ltd, Croydon, CR0 4YY
Printed in North America by CPI GPS partners

The author of this book does not dispense medical advice or prescribe the use of any technique
as a form of treatment for physical, emotional, or medical problems without the advice of a
physician, either directly or indirectly. The intent of the author is only to offer information of
a general nature to help you in your quest for emotional and spiritual well-being. In the event
you use any of the information in this book for yourself, which is your constitutional right, the
author and the publisher assume no responsibility for your actions.

We operate a distinctive and ethical publishing philosophy in
all areas of our business, from our global network of authors to
production and worldwide distribution.

"Love Dogs"

One night a man was crying,
"Allah! Allah!"
His lips grew sweet with the praising,
until a cynic said,
"So! I have heard you
calling out, but have you ever
gotten any response?"

The man had no answer to that.
He quit praying and fell into a confused sleep.

He dreamed he saw Khidr, the guide of souls,
in a thick, green foliage.
"Why did you stop praising?"
"Because I've never heard anything back."
"This longing you express is the return message."

The grief you cry out from
draws you toward union.

Your pure sadness
that wants help
is the secret cup.

Listen to the moan of a dog for its master.
That whining is the connection.

There are love dogs
no one knows the names of.
Give your life
to be one of them.

Jalal Al-Din Rumi

Contents

Preface

There is a growing population in our culture of individuals who are labeled *sensitive, dramatic, intense* — and there are many good reasons for these terms. These individuals deserve the love, care, and respect that others receive.

My book is for all of us who struggle, for those who love us, and for the culture at large. It is written from my own experience, having a doctorate in psychology, and working with many of these individuals. I was also born with the personality and orientation described in the following pages.

May this book be a hand and heart to hold you on your journey, while also helping therapists and loved ones to understand you. It is time for you to be met; only then can you meet yourself.

Acknowledgements

In writing this book, I want to first mention my developmental editor and friend, Brad Wetzler, and my editor, Skye Kerr Levy. After reading their efforts, I really liked my book. I want to thank my friendships who support me and are my lifeline. I also want to thank my brother for always offering encouragement and picking up the phone and my siblings and family. Of course, I want to thank my clients for endless hours of impact and heart. And thank you to an old mentor, Courtney Johnson; I will never forget your validation, acceptance, and your true understanding of therapy. And of course, thank you to my parents, who are the perfect characters for my complex psychic structure, and to my grandparents, who showed me generosity and that I am truly special.

Chapter 1

The Curse of Intensity

Crouched on all fours, she is naked and thin. Her hair is a fiery ball of tangles. She is bleeding and brown from the ground. Her only safety is the shackles and chains that bind her. She is a prisoner — a caged animal. She does not remember the fall from grace and or when she became bound, but the faint memory was not of something wrong. No, this felt like a natural urge, like Adam biting the apple. But it would not have mattered if she knew better; she was imprisoned forever with no way out. She was alone. The only hope of food or touch was from the men passing by on their journeys. Luring them in with her sweet smile and sensuality, she knew these men were her only hope for survival.

After weeks and months, the boredom set in and with it the realization that she was not free. Now she lunged and growled at the men as they passed by. Her bite drew blood and her sharp tongue drove them away. Once again alone, she would rest. Each man who passed was scared off by her attack. Man after man.

The pattern persisted until one day, while speaking to a wise bird who perched above her, she came to understand that the chains were her choice because she actually had the key. In fact, it was right in the shallow dirt hollow she had dug for herself to rest in at night. So why did she stay here — hungry, bloody, and ravaged?

The chains and her pain were more familiar than the world out there. Deep down, she was a gentle little girl who only knew love. This love was not just for men — it was the kind of love that transcended the physical realm, a love for all, and a love for herself: she *was* love.

But one day she got curious. Reluctantly, she released herself and set out through the vast forest that surrounded her. She was free. She was excited and terrified because, even though she *was* free, she did not know how to *be* free.

That is where her story begins. This is where our story begins. It is a story of a particular kind of person. This kind of person is intense. Perhaps a friend comes to mind who seems to always be longing to be seen as unique. Perhaps you have a family member who seems to feel things so deeply they almost get lost in these emotions. Or perhaps this person is you. Perhaps you suffer from anger and longing that threatens to burn you up from the inside with its heat. I call this person the Enneagram type Four or the person with a Borderline-style personality. Throughout this book, I will simplify the type to "the Four-Borderline". The psychic structure drives the experience of that particular kind of suffering. I will get into explaining the Enneagram Four more below, but for now know that both the Four type and those with Borderline style traits possess a particular psychic structure that drives them to frequent emotional overwhelm and a fluid sense of self. They often struggle with self-harm, substance abuse, self-hatred, interpersonal issues, and intense rage. These people make up a large percentage of the population in psychiatric wards and can create a lot of turmoil for themselves and their loved ones.

The journey for this type—for me, for you, or for a person you love—seems to begin with a lot of heartbreak. But I see that healing and reclamation of power and beauty is possible. That is what this book is about.

Many of us experience our day-to-day existence in a distorted way. We know this, and yet it is tough to change our own perception from our own point of view. We are born with a certain genetic code and then are nurtured, or not, by a parent or two, or caregivers who try their best. Society at large also influences the development of our psyche and beliefs. And the

4

whole of the cosmos infuses an energetic pattern into everything we become. Reality is not what it seems.

For a long time, I never took into consideration that beyond my upbringing and genetics, I had a personality and temperament influencing my entire experience. Even though my brother and I had been raised in the same family and society, we were completely different. I remember trying to explain the possibility of these differences between him and I with thoughts like: *Well, I am a girl. I had an infant trauma. I have more pressure from the media. I was drawn to the wayward kids,* and the list went on.

It was not until 2010, after I completed my doctorate in East/West psychology, that I stumbled on a system that explained these differences in my perception that made complete sense. I have been studying it ever since. It is called the Enneagram.

The Enneagram is an ancient map for identifying our point of view on life, which could be called our personality, and therefore our experience in life. Many in the Enneagram community believe we come into this world with a certain propensity for a particular distortion and/or point of view. As infants, when we experience the so-called fall from grace that happens as we differentiate from our caregivers and come into increasing contact with the world, we lose a particular orientation of the whole picture of the type that we were born to be. We can spend a lifetime trying to regain this sense of wholeness.

Miraculously, we are given the parents, the upbringing, and the life lessons to help us break free of our own distorted lens so that we can come back home to our Self. Self, as I use the term, can also be interchanged with God, essence, and consciousness. Through our childhoods, many of us are playing out our false selves—the tastes and behaviors we were conditioned to play out in order to survive all the layers of our surroundings, like our society, families, etc. For most of us, it is when we hit our early twenties that we start exploring ourselves and realize that we are not living in alignment with our own truth. We are far away from our Self. Once we do the work to become more aligned, we can start seeing where our attention goes, how we are staying fixated in our core wound or distortion, and how we are blocking our life force. Like it was for me, the Enneagram can be a wonderful map to start the process of really getting to know ourselves in a very clear way.

The Enneagram has its roots in ancient times. Armenian philosopher Ivanovitch Gurdjief, Oscar Ichazo, originator of Integral philosophy, and Claudio Naranjo, pioneer of the marriage of psychology and spirituality, brought the Enneagram to popularity as a personality system and it has slowly gained interest since the 1960s when it was first popularized. The Enneagram is a circle of nine points, nine ways of seeing the world, and each point contains within it a vice (a way we get stuck), virtue (something unique we can contribute), and a holy idea, which is that particular divine element we are separate from, and have special access to, from within our type. There are nine types: the One (the Reformer), the Two (the Helper), the Three (the Achiever), the Four (the Individualist), the Five (the Investigator), the Six (the Loyalist), the Seven (the Enthusiast), the Eight (the Challenger), the Nine (the Peacemaker). The Enneagram is a system through which we can get to know ourselves more deeply and also gain understanding of others' motivations. Think of it as a compassion tool. As a dynamic map, the Enneagram has wisdom regarding developmental growth, ways we can become healthy, and ways we can demonstrate stress. It has been said that this map can explain the full range of the human psyche and all movements of human behavior.

The premise is that if we can come to know ourselves deeply, then we can transcend the parts of ourselves that keep us from seeing our reality clearly. The ultimate goal, so to speak, is to fully see through the fixation and personality of our own

Enneagram type, while also embodying the essential energy of all the other eight types. And as this happens, we become a fully functioning and loving human.

The problem is that we forget that we are trapped in our distorted lens, and thus we tend to believe others see the world in the same way we do. We think others have the same needs, motivations, and preferences. This is far from the truth. Others have their own experience and they see reality through their own distorted point of view. And if we do not understand what others see, then this can cause continuous missing reality, assuming, and even blaming.

As a couples therapist, this kind of misunderstanding is so apparent in a new couple who has yet to learn the gift of the Enneagram system. For example, one partner may show their love by giving and not letting their partner know what they need. The other shows their partner love by being an expert and sharing their knowledge with their partner. If they do not have the insight that they are looking at life differently, they both can build up resentment that the other is not loving them, since they are not being taken care of in the way they would like to be.

Type Four

This book is a deep dive into one of the Enneagram numbers in particular. It can be said that of all the types, there is one that has a more challenging time growing and seeing through their limitations than the others. Yes, this type is the Four—also known as the Individualist, the Romantic, or the Artist. I am all too familiar with this type; as a therapist, I specialize in treating Fours, some of my closest friends are Fours, and I am a Four.

The path of type Four is a difficult one due to a few fundamental reasons.

The first is the Four's negativity bias towards reality: the cup is half full and something is always seen as missing. The something-is-missing applies to every person around them, almost every situation they are in, and includes themselves as well.

The second challenge is self-absorption. Fours see themselves as having personal significance and an identity that is special and unique.

And the real doozy is the "deadly sin" of the Four (each Enneagram type is associated with a sin as well as a holy idea— more on that later) which is envy. Fours are always envying another person, place, or thing, and comparing themselves with that ideal. Most everything in life is experienced through this lens of envy and perfection. *If I were prettier and smarter, then I would be happy. If this man liked me, then I would be worthy and lovable.* Picture a character like Eeyore in *Winnie the Pooh*; this glum negativity is the way we Fours often experience life. Life does not seem fair and somehow it seems like this is our dharma, it is inevitable, it is our sad lot in life.

Within our culture, Four personalities are in the minority, thought to be at only three percent of all the personality types. Thus, their motivations are not valued as much in our current production-obsessed and success-oriented society. In short, these beautiful individuals usually feel displaced.

This book is dedicated to all of us who struggle on this particular Four path as a way of saying "I understand. I see you. I am with you." As we progress more into in the next chapter, remember that the strength and beauty of type Fours is immense and potent.

When I first landed in my own type, after trying on the two others which happen to be the types I lean into with regards to health and stress (we will talk more about this later), I started to really, finally, understand how I viewed the world. Like a warm, welcoming blanket, this system gave me permission to finally start being me.

I had always felt somewhat like an alien. As I started to be myself, I attracted mostly type Four personalities in my practice.

Over the last fifteen years or so, I have worked intimately with about a hundred or more of this type—individually and in couples. Of course, people come to therapy because they are struggling, so I spent over a decade working with the more entrenched type Fours. The pattern that I saw was that these struggling Fours were also often people with a Borderline Personality Disorder (BPD) or Cyclothymic Bipolar diagnosis. As I mentioned above, even if you do not have the clinical, official diagnosis of BPD, this style of reacting to and being in the world lives on a spectrum and many of us can relate or see qualities of this style in ourselves—especially when we are very triggered by an intimate partner. Fluctuations from fantasy to anger are pretty common. There is often a desperate attempt to feel needed while at the same time a feeling of terror and the desire to push others away.

Although there is a stigma in the field of therapy against Borderline style behaviors as they can be so intense and can often be turned against the therapist, these individuals were easy for me to work with as I had the same psychic structure as they did and my nervous system was calmer—or frozen, possibly—than another therapist's might be. And most importantly I heard the deep and resonant cry for help in these people who wanted to understand themselves and be themselves.

This broke my heart. I spent many hours over a decade trying to save each and every one of these clients. Midnight phone calls, emails expressing a want to die, hospital visits, dramatic events to get attention—the list went on and on. With each passing week and many maintenance calls, I continued to reflect their lovability with validation and care until they were able to witness a sliver of themselves on their own. Slowly and surely, their psychic split became more and more integrated so they could enjoy life's offerings—or at least some of them.

As I worked, I dove deep into the literature of psychology to learn everything possible about Borderline traits. With my research, the Enneagram, and my own internal understanding and empathy of this particular human dilemma, I felt like I was someone suitable for the job. I produced a documentary to help spread the word that there is hope for those diagnosed with Borderline Personality Disorder.

And yes—over the years it became clear to me that this style of suffering is intense and can have negative outcomes for therapists. Boundaries and clear eyes are needed. Still I happily work mostly with Four-type personalities with Borderline traits that find difficulty in relationships, career, use various forms of substances, and we focus on helping them learn to embody a sense of self. Because, in my opinion, a deep unchanging *sense of self* is everything.

I know because I can finally rest in me too—well, most of the time. This integrated sense of self is the profound shift that I see healthy, prospering Fours and people with Borderline traits finding peace through. I give credit to the Enneagram, my teachers, and my relationships for being able to enjoy life more deeply than I ever did before.

The following pages are about how to find this peace and about how to be yourself. This book is for those I love, myself included, and for those who love us. And my prayer is that the culture at large may finally learn to integrate our beauty and depth in its fabric, just as we must learn to do for ourselves.

Chapter 2

Meet the Four-Borderline Type

The Four-Borderline Personality

Do you have a friend who always sees the glass as half empty? For them, what is *missing* is always in sight, not what is there? Or maybe *you* are this person! This psyche compares to others and feels a sense of envy with most everything. The longing that hums beneath it all is: if I have what you have, I will be happy and will not feel like something is missing. The way we Four-Borderlines see the world is that something is lacking, and we must find ourselves within these holes. Our attention is usually on comparing ourselves to almost everyone and everything. As such, the vice of the Four (and each Enneagram type has one) is the vice of envy. We connect our lovability to how we are doing compared to others—our culture, our industry, our peers, and our judgment.

What gives us our personality? We all have one. There are so many ways of defining, viewing, and explaining that concept, but for our purposes we can think of our personality as the outcomes of the inherited traits, lived experiences, the strengths and struggles, the insight and the neurosis with which we interface with the world. There are many ways in and many lenses to view personality typology through. Let us explore some common psychological language that can be applied to the Four-Borderline and then deepen our understanding of the Four within the Enneagram tradition.

There are many well-respected, formal personality assessments. You may have taken some of these tests at work or done a self-assessment online. How does the Four-Borderline type we are talking about fit into these assessment models? According to the personality profile Meyers-Briggs, which sprung from Carl Jung's typology, we could say the Four is an INFP or INFJ, which stands for Introverted, iNtuitive, Feeling, and Perceiving (or Judging).

The *DSM*, the mental-health diagnostic manual, could be seen as capturing the extreme of what the type Four can go to: Borderline Personality Disorder and/or Cyclothymic Bipolar, as I mentioned before.

In archetypal terms, we can see Four-type women as the Damsel in Distress and the Maiden—caught in a younger place, seeking salvation from the Other. Greek Gods like Aphrodite and Venus also come to mind.

To me, all of this adds up to create the impression that the Four-Borderline is thoughtful, deep, sensitive, artistic, dramatic, bold, emotional, and oriented toward their own experience.

Is a picture starting to form in your mind of this type? It is a person displaying Western concepts of femininity to an extreme, coming across as highly emotional, dramatic, and victim-like. This individual can also appear to be highly self-absorbed in their subjective, personal experience—as if life is happening *to* them. So every conversation, every experience, and most ruminating thoughts are about "me." Without a solid sense of self and unstable emotions, life can be experienced as if with no skin—which naturally creates a kind of constant pain and sensitivity that creates self-absorption.

A. H. Almaas, founder of the Diamond Approach, articulated a concept within Enneagram studies of each type having a "holy idea." This may sound religious, but I think what he means by it is that we each have a central wisdom that contributes to the complete insight of the whole of the Enneagram circle—the whole of humans as a unity. For type Four, this holy idea is "Holy Origin." This is the paradoxical flip side of the profound, dark, hole of lack and loss that Fours often feel sits at the very center of their being. Their core belief and behaviors are compensatory to fill in this deep hole and loss—the disconnection from the Holy

Origin, connection with which would be the exact opposite. (The concept of Holy Origin is discussed later.)

As a way to soothe the potential deep drop into depression that such a lacking, envious, or comparative mindset can create, enter the "fantasy life" of the Four. This fantasizing is another defense mechanism, and it creates a relentless pursuit to be unique so as not to feel ordinary, so as not to feel lacking, so as not to feel melancholy. Fantasy pulls one out of mundane reality and into the desired life, seemingly just out of reach. Remembering the past or longing for the future allows the feelings and emotions to be accessible. It motivates behavior— sometimes good and other times bad. It gives a sense of beauty and illusion to everyday life. But the issue with fantasy is that it creates a dissociated state. If our ultimate goal is to enjoy innate peace and joy, then we are manufacturing a state by putting our attention on fantasy and not living in the world as our embodied selves.

The main life purpose of the Four is for personal significance: to be seen, to be special, to be unique. So there is a lot of time and energy put into testing others to see if they understand one's uniqueness. For a Four, everything is felt deeply, and life can be lived as a tragic love story. Melancholy is the main fixation, like an old familiar friend, something to curl up with on those less than exciting days. Because Fours long to feel special and that their lives are especially meaningful, daily tasks can feel mundane and are thus pushed to the side and overlooked.

And finally, an emptiness, or a lack of a sense of self, is something that all of us Fours seem to have in common. On one hand, this emptiness can allow us to rest in an expansive and open place. Because there is a depth of experience without a solid sense of self, we can easily feel very connected with spirit and the universe. And on the other hand, this does not allow for a felt sense of being grounded or rooted.

In fact, of all qualities and orientations I have illuminated so far, I would say this central sense of *groundlessness* is the most difficult to heal and often becomes the largest obstruction to well-being.

When a Four-Borderline Is Triggered

What triggers a Four-Borderline? And what are the typical reactive behaviors? I have sat in many groups with many Four-Borderlines, I have many clients that are Four-Borderlines, and I am a Four-Borderline type; I consistently hear the primary trigger is *feeling dismissed*.

The dismissal can be felt in many different arenas, and the feeling underlying it all is "you do not value me or care about me." Feeling or being dismissed is the Achilles heel of the Four-Borderline. Anytime we do not feel heard, understood, or are ignored, the experience can trigger something deep inside, which often erupts as anger or rage, or we become moody and withdrawn. Underneath that is a painful feeling which stems from not getting the attunement and validation that was needed as a baby or a child or all the times we dismissed our own selves—our feelings, needs, and wants. There is also a body reaction that goes along with this trigger for some of us. Mine includes an overall body sensation with a vague and dizzy kind of feeling. I have heard other Four-Borderlines describe it in a similar way. When the trigger is really big, it can also produce a pain that feels like a hole going straight through the heart.

The Healthy Four and Holy Origin

Given all these challenges, what is the way out? What is the path for the Four-Borderline to become more in balance within themselves and in the world? Part of the way out is to identify less with these intense reactive feelings and begin to see that the personality is not *who* we are. Because in explaining the experience of the Four-Borderline, it is important to note that being this type is not a negative diagnosis—there are levels of development within Four-ness, just as there are within all the Enneagram types. The more identified a person is in their personality, the unhealthier they are. For example, someone who feels dismissed may be paralyzed by the experience and may feel that *no one will be there for me* and that *no one loves me.* Even perhaps that life is too difficult to live. A healthier, growing Four person may feel the dismissal, but then remember how much they enjoy their life and their own relationship with themselves. Such growth and development lessens the ego fixation and can dramatically shift one's experience and attitude. Thankfully, we have a choice when it comes to growth and healing.

Remember, the Four-Borderline's deepest positive connection is to the truth of their Holy Origin: the core perfect, completeness that exists at the center of us all. Thus, the literature states that the Four-Borderline in its highest form possesses a sense of equanimity and joy—the kind of joyful equanimity that can only spring from a deep, abiding sense of a core connection to one's holy origin. The drama shifts to a calm state of "all is well" and being is more objective, less subjective, and thus more balanced and stable. The journey of life is devoted to feeling this sense of the deepest connection. From here springs a sense of meaningful joy that is the deepest positive quality of a Four.

Four-Borderlines are soul-dwellers and truth-tellers. When a Four is feeling healthy there is an objective quality of being compassionate, expressive, and supportive. When we can validate ourselves, we feel our specialness as an intrinsic power—we hold magic, fun, and curiosity that is attractive and potent. We are constantly looking beneath the surface of things to find the meaning and to add our influence. There are so many famous Enneagram Fours who have transferred this sensitivity and creativity into the world. Many artists, musicians, actors, and dancers have this orientation. Johnny Depp, Vincent Van

Gogh, Bob Dylan, Joni Mitchell, Meryl Streep, Prince, and Kurt Cobain were or are all Fours. If you follow the work of these artists, they all have incredible powers of expressing the soulful, deep, watery darkness of the human experience, allowing all of us to touch into more of our own emotions and to appreciate the humanness of life through their work. Our world would definitely be a less colorful place without these rare beings.

Four-Borderlines are sensitive to everything in our surroundings, including beauty. Most things need to be just right—lighting, sound, our connection with another person, another person's energy, organization of space, and the list goes on. When this sensitivity is used for good, this type really benefits from being in understanding relationships with others so that the Four-Borderline can practice not taking things so personally but also engaging with needs outside of themselves. As much of our hurt comes from feeling dismissed or unvalued, seeing something outside of ourselves is extremely relieving. And it allows us Four-Borderlines to get the connection we deserve because we love connection and to be valued. And when we know a little about how someone else sees the world, we may be better able to understand what we need to say or do to get the connection we so value.

Developmental Stages for Type Four-Borderline

As hard as it can be to be a Four-Borderline, there are stages of development and ways they can learn to function better—just like there are for any type. Within each Enneagram type, there is a developmental range, a spectrum of being, from the most identified with the ego and dysfunction at worst, to being the least identified with the ego and happily functioning at best. Many people do not reach the high points in their lifetime, since these states of full development can perhaps be seen as being similar to spiritual awakening. We all usually slide up and down a few levels within our experience. However, with deep commitment to change, we can achieve a new set-point of experience. A new normal.

Part of my work is to help people suffering see the limitations and pain that identifying with their ego structure—their firm opinions, reactivity, and habitual thinking—is causing for them. As their emotions are witnessed and they are given space to process, I see a loosening of their attachment to themselves as they have previously understood themselves and an opening up into other possible ways of being and viewing themselves. This is development.

Enneagram teachers Russ Hudson and Don Richard Riso articulated these levels of development as a way to see the qualities and structure of each type. With less fixation, we can see clearly and our essence can express itself in its natural way. The more fixated we are, the more we are in our conditioning and we cannot see through our limitations. Remember that each type has their own levels, but for the sake of detailing the journey of the Four type, below is Don Richard Riso and Russ Hudson's articulation from *The Wisdom of the Enneagram* (1999) of what the dysfunction and functionality can look like:

"**Healthy Levels. Level 1:** Profoundly creative, expressing the personal and the universal, possibly in a work of art. Inspired, self-renewing and regenerating: able to transform all their experiences into something valuable; self-creative. **Level 2:** Self-aware, introspective, on the "search for self," aware of feelings and inner impulses. Sensitive and intuitive both to self and others; gentle, tactful, compassionate. **Level 3:** Highly personal, individualistic, 'true to self.' Self-revealing, emotionally honest, humane. Ironic view of self and life; can be serious and funny, vulnerable, and emotionally strong.

Average Levels. Level 4: Take an artistic, romantic orientation to life, creating a beautiful, aesthetic environment to cultivate and prolong personal feelings. Heighten reality through fantasy, passionate feelings, and the imagination. **Level 5:** To stay in touch with feelings, they interiorize everything, taking everything personally, but become self-absorbed and introverted, moody and hypersensitive, shy and self-conscious, unable to be spontaneous or to 'get out of themselves.' Stay withdrawn to protect their self-image and to buy time to sort out feelings. **Level 6:** Gradually think that they are different from others and feel that they are exempt from living as everyone else does. They become melancholy dreamers, disdainful, decadent, and sensual, living in a fantasy world. Self-pity and envy of others leads to self-indulgence, and to becoming increasingly impractical, unproductive, effete, and precious.

Unhealthy Levels. Level 7: When dreams fail, become self-inhibiting and angry at self, depressed and alienated from self and others, blocked and emotionally paralyzed. Ashamed of self, fatigued, and unable to function. **Level 8:** Tormented by delusional self-contempt, self-reproaches, self-hatred, and morbid thoughts; everything is a source of torment. Blaming others, they drive away anyone who tries to help them. **Level 9:** Despairing, feel hopeless and become self-destructive, possibly abusing alcohol or drugs to escape. In the extreme: emotional breakdown or suicide is likely."
Riso and Hudson

If you want to dive even deeper into all this, there is also a theory that each type follows a specific path when they are stressed or dysfunctional. Under stress, type Fours can move toward type Two and exhibit the unhealthy version of that type. Russ Hudson and Don Richard Riso articulated the unhealthy levels of the Two as:

"**Level 7**: Can be manipulative and self-serving, instilling guilt by telling others how much they owe them and make them suffer. Abuse food and medication to 'stuff feelings' and get sympathy. Undermine people, making belittling, disparaging remarks. Extremely self-deceptive about their motives and how aggressive and/or selfish their behavior is. **Level 8**: Domineering and coercive; feel entitled to get anything they want from others: the repayment of old debts, money, sexual favors. **Level 9**: Able to excuse and rationalize what they do since they feel abused and victimized by others and are bitterly resentful and angry. Somatization of their aggressions results in chronic health problems as they vindicate themselves by 'falling apart' and burdening others." **Riso and Hudson**

I see, feel, and have experienced strong validation of this line of thinking—that the very dysfunctional Four will act like an unhealthy Two.

Type Four within the Whole Enneagram Circle

The nine Enneagram types are often grouped into three groups of three, making up the three heart/feeling types, the three head/thinking types, and the three body/instinctive types. These three groupings are called the three "centers."

Type Four lives in the heart center of the Enneagram (along with types Two and Three). Research by David Daniels and others say the heart center lives in the limbic and mammalian part of the brain. This is the area of emotion including connection, touch, bonding, and an overall sense of *am I loved?* When there is a disruption of this area, there can be much distress. The individual will take action to do whatever it takes to not feel the pain of the disconnection and the separation from love.

The other Enneagram centers are the head center and the body center. The head center is reflected in the neo-cortex, the area of the brain used to learn, know, understand, and analyze. When type Five, Six, and Seven individuals are afraid, unsure, or threatened, there will be a lot of energy focused on *seeing* something. There is an experience of *thinking about* your feelings and sensations. It can be very tricky for the types in the head center to know whether they are living in their pseudo-feelings or actually *meeting* their feelings and processing them. Needless to say, this access to visceral emotions is easy-peasy for the Four.

The types in the body/instinctive center—types Eight, Nine, and One—act from their guts. This center is reflected in the reptilian part of the brain, which is involved with feeling safe at the visceral, physical level. When others take up too much space or power, the types in this center can feel challenged, off-center, and angry.

If you consider now where the Four sits in relation to all these centers and the other types, what emerges is that the Four sits at the edge of the heart/feeling center as it is right next to the Five, where the head/thinking center begins. In this way, the Four has special access to thinking; us Fours use thinking to conjure up our deep emotions—whether it is to relive past experiences or to long for what is missing and may never be. There is thought that goes into almost every feeling for the Four. *How do I think I feel about what has happened?* is more descriptive of the Four experience than just a simple *I feel*. The body is usually left as an afterthought (which makes sense given how far away the Four sits from the body/instinct center), and sensations are not usually felt. It also makes sense if you consider that the body center is the most earthly, grounded, and in the Four's view, mundane—a dreaded word to the Four!

Thus to balance out the strong presence of the feeling and thinking energies for the Four, Enneagram wisdom would suggest that balance, healing, and wholeness would be created for the Four through inviting more of the balancing energy of body work: the awareness and the attention of *how does my body feel right now?* Or *what does my body want?* We will dive more into healing in later chapters. It is a necessary part of the journey for the Four personality to experience more of their objective head and full body so that balance can be restored between all their centers and parts of their brain. When all parts are utilized in a systematic way for what they are intended for, the nervous system can come to a resting place.

In the next chapter, we will continue this study of the Four-Borderline personality type with my life story, evocative interviews, and my clinical observations about the personal, nuanced, and powerful journey of suffering and healing for this type.

Chapter 3

My Painful, Beautiful Journey

Childhood Traumas

My journey is typical to the many Four-Borderline clients I have sat with over the past ten years. There are a few key and fascinating markers that most of us share—a thread of shared experience that you will see in my story here and in theirs in the following chapter.

*Many of us had infant surgeries, which likely altered our nervous systems to be more sensitive or more frozen/traumatized than others.

*Many of us experienced a primary caretaker that was not emotionally validating or available to help soothe our sensitive system or bring our frozen nervous system back online.

*Many of us experienced abandonment. Perhaps one of our parents left our home or came and went frequently, leaving us feeling alone in the unpredictability.

*Many of us resorted to performing to be shown love in the family.

*Many of us have never felt validated for all that we are.

*Many of us fear abandonment with our entire being.

The first six weeks after my birth foreshadowed the following decades. I began projectile vomiting from the first moment I was given breast milk. I had pyloric stenosis: the opening of my stomach was closed. This is usually only found in males of Jewish ancestry, and I am not a male. As a firstborn, I cannot imagine what my parents went through as they carted me from hospital to hospital to figure out what was wrong with their Exorcist baby. It doesn't surprise me that I was bulimic through my teens and occasionally in my twenties, and I can also interpret I am probably not the best at letting in nourishment from people and food.

When there was finally a surgery performed, my dad was present to make sure the incision would not be the cause of bikini shame for the rest of my days. These days my three-inch incision seems to somewhat blend in with my fifty-year-old belly. However, I did spend a lot of time staring in the mirror at this scar as a girl—as if somehow without it my life would be different.

All went well with the surgery, and I stayed in the hospital for the first six weeks of life. I do not have much recollection of childhood, however whether a dream or true, I do have a vivid first memory of lying under a very bright light.

As I have come to know as a therapist, you are not set up for a healthy attachment system when you have been sliced open and hospitalized for the first few weeks of your initial time on the planet. There are times when I go through break-ups that I swear I am back in the hospital room—I feel abandoned at a primitive level that is hard to put into words.

As it is for many of us, my parents were not the model of a perfect relationship, or even a particularly healthy one. Mine were divorced when I was ten. It seems that event did not affect my brother as much as me; he is married with four daughters. I will never forget being at the dinner table when my parents got into an argument and my dad crushed a wine glass with his bare hands and threw a biscuit into the kitchen, which almost hit me on its path. A few hours later, I was in my parents' room and heard that my dad was leaving. A story that has arisen in most of my personal therapy over the last thirty years is the moment I firmly held onto my dad's ankle as he dragged me across the floor on his way out. Holding tight, I cried, "daddy, don't leave me."

As a teen, I would write poetry in my bedroom while also talking on the phone late into the night with a boy from school.

Hoping, praying, bargaining: *would he be the one who picks me?* I was always thinking about what was missing, even if a boy was right there. My father leaving created a pattern of fearing every man would leave. At times, I self-sabotaged so they had no choice but to leave. At the same time, I was internalizing many messages from my mom that I did not need a man and that they were "like a piece of furniture."

Neither of my parents knew anything about parenting or how to create a happy and healthy human being. There was a lot of emphasis on activities and *doing* and very little emphasis on who I was as a person and how I experienced the world. As a teen, I became bulimic and mildly anorexic, which was no doubt my attempt to control all the out-of-control feelings I had inside that I could not make sense of. I also began self-harming, which finally made me feel alive. Other than those two secret developments, I performed well in school, was popular, and lived as best I could in accordance with my parents' messages and the culture I lived within.

Midlife Searching and Hard Lessons

After college was when the wheels started coming off. While I had all of these traumatic experiences, I did not fully experience my Four-Borderline-ness until my twenties. Prior to that, it seemed to be masked by my achievement in athletics, academics, and socializing. It was not until I moved from my hometown of Chicago to San Francisco that my unbridled emotions and unstable behavior emerged. At the same time, I kept my attention on the beauty of my surroundings and continued to be touched by human experience. My personal significance captured most of my attention. I had a myriad of boyfriends, who, at some point, I would turn to as a life raft for my own survival. I remember feeling on multiple occasions that I would literally die if I did not have consistent contact or if there was some kind of rupture between us.

I tried so hard to be self-sufficient and independent, but without knowing what to ask for and how to soothe my emotions, I was a walking time bomb. All it took was for my boyfriend to go away for the weekend, and I became unhinged with the loneliness, desperation, and what I perceived to be rejection. I did not have the capacity to step back to see the relationship from his point of view. There was a lot of additional anger that built up in not feeling seen or having my needs met. There were numerous times I had an episode—which basically was an altered state of mind—in which I would scream, cry, and say very critical things.

I also invested a tremendous amount of energy into my career. Within the span of a few years, I tried many things, including being a bartender, a publishing assistant, a clothing wholesaler, a school teacher, and taking many temp jobs to get a feel for various industries. There was always a feeling that the position was not quite right. I struggled, and still do to this day, to land on something that felt exactly like *me*. One of the ultimate pursuits of a Four-Borderline is to find personal significance, so this has been my cross to bear. Furthermore, there is a lot of internal pressure to be unique and special, so it is not enough to do *something*; a lot of self-criticism can come from being less than perfect and unique.

Beyond men, there was also a heightened sensitivity to people and the world around me. I remember business dinners about twenty years ago that would actually leave me feeling like I was a shaved sheep with no skin. Everything would penetrate, and I would soak up the entire night—including alcohol—and then wake up for work the next day to begin again. At this time, I was in upper management as a vice president. I am not sure how I made it.

After my mother passed away, my life in the business world stopped making sense to me. I wanted to help people beyond doing the next business deal that did not seem to deliver any value. After taking a sabbatical and then finally quitting, I headed to Telluride to sit on a mountain and think. I decided to enter a counseling psychology program.

It was discovering the Enneagram that finally gave me some understanding and relief more than anything else I had ever encountered. When I landed on my type, it was as if I finally had the secret formula for why I felt like a unicorn in a land of horses my entire life. I was sensitive, yet intense. I desired to belong, whilst holding a strong need to be unique and different. My experience was that I felt almost everything much deeper than others seemed to.

I was learning, studying, and healing, yet the pattern of emotional swings and numerous men lasted throughout my thirties and forties.

When my longest relationship—of four years—came to an end, I decided to start my PhD in East-West Psychology. But I had some time before the program began. How to fill it?

Years prior, I had met a man in Costa Rica who owned a healing center in Delray Beach, Florida. I felt I was on my way to learn how to run a healing center and we reconnected. He had a grant from the government, which intrigued me. So across the country to Florida I flew.

One day while there, I walked into a juice bar and a tall, handsome, and extremely friendly man was making the juice. He said he had never seen me before and we talked about my interest in East-West psychology and my internship at the healing center. He invited me to a satsang—a gathering with a realized being—where he lived.

A few nights later, I took him up on his invitation. There, I found a house with a pool, mediation, yoga, and a group of very good-looking spiritual seekers. It was not until I met with the guru, whose name was I Am, that I found what I was looking for. I told him that the ashram would be my last stop. I had searched for happiness everywhere and could not find it—until now. I will never forget at that very moment that I told him this, a white light came from the window over his shoulder and penetrated my heart. I was sold.

I went back to San Francisco, put my stuff in storage, and drove cross-country.

Daily life at the ashram had most of my favorite things: dance, mediation, yoga, vegetarian food, discourse on enlightenment, spiritual movies, and interesting people, including a new boyfriend. We also had basic karma yoga chores. For a good month or two, it seemed like Utopia. And then some things started to feel off. I did not like the way the guru spoke to some of the women. We were becoming restricted about working and traveling outside of the home.

I also noticed I was getting very sweaty after each lunch. I was dropping weight from all the exercise and eating well. My perception was getting a little bizarre—like seeing everything in pixels with space in between. I started to experience my thoughts as if they were getting projected onto the screen of my reality. I must have been worried about my boyfriend noticing good-looking woman, because I started seeing supermodels everywhere. Everywhere. Even in the Florida suburbs. Even in the grocery store.

I still feel uncertain as to what exactly happened. Was I drugged? Was I meditating too much and not getting enough sleep? Was I finding the truth of reality? Who knows. But I did find at that crazy place a visceral knowing of *me*, of I, of the substrate of reality that is unchangeable, reliable, and stable. To this day, I can still locate that same place in me. So, I guess it wasn't all for nothing.

But I became more and more paranoid living at the ashram. The guy I was dating no longer wanted to be my boyfriend. I started planning my exit. I gathered my things when the guru was out of the house—which rarely happened. A few members were teaching yoga and one of the guys was by the front door.

With my bags, I pushed the guy out of the way and ran towards my car.

Feeling really unstable, I ended up driving back to Chicago to spend some time in the land of Midwestern stability and normalcy. It took me more than a few months to integrate back into reality; I felt like I had been brainwashed. Another attempt at consistent happiness had failed—although I will never forget that glimpse of my unwavering self.

My next biggest teacher was my breast "C." I do not use the word c.a.n.c.e.r. Ironically, my little calcifications—also called DCIS (Ductal Carcinoma in Situ)—appeared in a mammogram at the ashram. I had no idea what lay ahead. I was called into a room to see my x-ray scans marked with a big, black circle around these little breadcrumbs. At this point, I had let my COBRA insurance end from my last corporate job, so I was on my own with healthcare. I did a good job ignoring the new scare until I got back to San Francisco from the Midwest.

Then I began the wild "C" goose chase: seeing oncologists, pathologists, radiologists, and surgeons to get each of their opinions on a very rigid formula of treatment—mastectomy with radiation and Tamoxifen. My diagnosis, which apparently 50,000 women per year share, is actually being reconsidered; they talk about taking the "C" out of DCIS. So I tried to pair the western and eastern worlds, seeking answers before I lopped off both breasts.

At first I elected to have a lumpectomy to scoop out the little calcifications and rejected radiology and Tamoxifen. At that time, I still had a potential window of childbearing and the drug would have wiped out any chance at having a healthy baby. In addition to the lumpectomy, I began to consult eastern treatment. For example, I spoke with a well-known doctor who had lived out of the country since the U.S. government had started to harass him into shutting down his practice. I also went to see a man named something like Ajanous in Malibu to do a raw meat diet and get my irises scanned. He had published books about his treatment of "C," and after reading my iris scores said he would suggest, "Cutting off my doctor's breasts or penis."

The eastern treatment continued with Dr. Miki Shima, a known Oriental Medicine doctor, to do oxygen-replacement therapy along with a strict diet.

My favorite and most bizarre of all the treatments was from my close friend's husband who worked as a physicist with a lab on Stanford's campus. He took a sample of my hair and nails and then put them in test tubes with liquid and shot a powerful beam through them. The energy source was from "another dimension" that he had discovered that would help rid our world of "C." When he would zap my test tubes, I could definitely feel it from afar.

I will also never forget one western surgeon rolling her eyes at all of this and showing me pictures of people who had let their "C" spread. I saw big bulging, bloody tumors.

All these theatrics went on for about eight years in total. But one day I was walking the path in Marin and contemplating life, like I often did, and it dawned on me to just end the madness and get a boob job. I know that sounds crass, but I could not take away the fear of western medicine that said I was going to die or grow big scary tumors any longer. I decided that if I did not know for sure if I actually had "C," at least I could live the rest of my days with nice breasts and be somewhat free from the fear—or so I thought.

(Fast forward through three surgeries, one requiring an expander to stretch the skin. Not at all comfortable and very tough to explain to my new boyfriend at the time. Even after six weeks sedentary between each surgery, I am left with uneven breasts. So much for my nice boob job. However there has been no "C" — unless it comes back. Luckily, there is a very small percentage since all the flesh was removed. I still get regular mammograms and MRIs.)

Life back in San Francisco had not just been about the journey with "C." I was doing more and more work with clients with Borderline Personality Disorder and Borderline characteristics. And I was learning a lot about myself and the journey of other Fours. These were individuals who had a point of view similar to me, though to a more extreme degree. They would often be highly dramatic, demonstrating some self-harm along with suicidal ideation. I would soak up their need for my validation and connection and would literally come home with no *me* to feed or speak from. For many years, I felt like I was doing meaningful work, but that I did not exist. I was doing my best to treat these sensitive souls, but was disappearing into the work.

Healing in Boulder

I decided to leave that life behind and move to Boulder, Colorado. My original inspiration was to leave behind another failed romance with someone I had been convinced was my life partner and my final surgery of the breast reconstruction fix was complete. Boulder seemed like a smaller San Francisco, that had strong connections with spirituality, nature, technology, and community. I also wanted to heal psychologically from my breast "C" by being away from all the hospitals and all the memories I had in the Bay Area. And the driven, image-focused culture of the Bay Area had worn thin for me. I was definitely running away from a lot — but I believe there was a healthy desire in me to walk towards something more natural, more grounded, more me.

My suffering in love did not end in Boulder. There were many more years of dating, with many relationships lasting for a month or two. After every one, I would go through a forty-eight-hour hell that entailed lots of phone calls with therapist friends, pacing around my house, deep existential heartache, and sensations I will never forget. Every time, each break up was like a cannon blowing through my entire chest for hours on end, leaving me feeling like a hollow, empty shell.

I also looked around Boulder at all its offerings. I attended Dharma Ocean meditations, an open house or two at the Shambala Center, many movement meditations, and sat with various practitioners in town. Without being closer to any sense of additional joy, I decided to start my own group. I talked to two other friends who had been steeped in the spiritual circuit and our first group was held about one year ago. One friend had been with Gangaji for years and the other had been with a lot of the self-inquiry gurus, Zen, and then found his deeper self through a psychedelic guide. Our group would eventually grow to thirteen members who meet every week and explore all things to do with self. We are attempting to strip the spiritual language out of the path and just trying to embody self as much as each of us can. We do a check in, have a discourse on ways to more fully embody self, and then do exercises to experience and express this phenomenon. It has been the most consistent and influential group I have ever attended and now, thankfully, I can say I have a community in Boulder. It seems to me like the more we can come from ourselves and be mirrored by those to whom we can really attune, the more we have a chance at seeing through all the self-conditioned layers.

This life as a Four-Borderline type has not all been bad and sad. There is a way I see the world that is not just sensate or things-as-they-appear. I see the world as if I am in a movie and could be any character. I see the humanness and subtle expressions of others. This rich drama makes life fun and worth living; for me, to experience life any other way would feel ordinary. And feeling ordinary is the antithesis of how I want to feel and who I want to be. *Please, dear God, do not let me feel ordinary!* And yet, I know that to embrace being ordinary is part of my spiritual path and a way deeper into belonging. The paradox here is either painful or beautiful, depending on how I hold it.

My life experience and who I am enables me to help see others who experience the world in a similar way to me. As a therapist, professor, group leader, and someone who pursued many creative endeavors in the healing space, I feel I have a healing path to offer. Having walked this path, I can truly and deeply celebrate all my clients' feelings, all their beauty, and all their authenticity. I can love them until they see how to love themselves.

There is hope. I can honestly say now that I can lose a man and not have my world torn apart. I can state my needs and can accept the ebb and flow of relationships, while always having myself. I have myself now. This makes a world of difference. In the words of my mother, "I do not need a man"; it is finally true.

With fifty-five right around the corner, I can finally say I am healed. Perfect, no; a strong sense of equanimity, yes. Most of my days are filled with a sense of *all is well*. I really like who I am. I treat myself with love and care. And I feel utilized by the universe to support humans like me in finding their own way to self-love.

So what is next? I am addicted to the search. Life partner? Nope. I surrendered to letting go of that concept. More aligned career? I am now teaching, lead supervision groups, have a full client practice, am developing an app, and writing this book. Perhaps I can take a deep breath: I may be mostly aligned with my life purpose. If there is nothing left to seek or find, then what? Now, it is all about growing, building, experiencing, and expressing myself in all my flavors with each new experience. To deeply feel myself and others and all of life. And I know that an encounter with another tragedy or heartache may throw me into darkness. I pray I may learn within the steady hum of normal life.

My biggest lesson was seeing that I played resonant and small to make sure someone liked me and did not leave. It worked. But when I finally expressed a need, I often felt I was not acknowledged for who I was or what I said. When my request was not cared for, I either got dramatic, despaired, or collapsed. Then I would run, but all I wanted was to be held and soothed. I was once again that little baby in the hospital, longing for the steady, loving, presence of someone who would stay unconditionally.

After going through this pattern over and over again with business partnerships, romantic relationships, and friendships, I am more aware. I am home. I am here to say, "Hey, no, oops wait, ummm, not quite … yes, that is what I need." And I also now understand that although I have a request, it does not necessarily mean that anyone is contracted to complete my request.

The Unconditional Love of Dogs

I have a memory from childhood about the day my border collie, Robbie, was taken away. There was no warning. One day some people came to our house and took him. I remember crying for what seemed like days. It was the first stab to my heart as Robbie was ripped from my arms. My first love left.

Today, I am sitting on my couch with my dog, Bella, as she waits patiently for her morning walk.

The first time I laid eyes on Bella was at a household in Colorado Springs. She was with a big litter and, as I met all the puppies, she was the one to grip my leg and look at me with big, longing eyes. My decision was made. She came to me wearing a very tight shirt that she was outgrowing quickly that said "who rescued who"? I laughed. I did not know the depth of that message until after this magical fur-angel landed in my life.

She is my mirror and my companion. And she seems to display most of my own qualities—protectiveness, coquettish, sweet, feisty, agile, and easily bored. We have a perfect marriage: she tells me what she needs and I do the same. With each man that comes to our house, she bats her eyes and pokes their arm with her paw, seeming to say, "Okay, now it is time to hold my hand, silly," or, "Okay, I am going to go chew on a bone now because you are annoying me." My favorite is that when she feels excluded from a conversation she will whip her head from side to side, letting out a short growl.

The most I have learned from us is that to take care of another being and to receive that care is the recipe for life. I make sure that she eats, pees, poops, exercises, and gets many belly rubs. And I receive her inquisitive glance, her paw on my arm, her warm body nuzzled next to mine, her lick on my lips, and her fierce protection. She is my Bell. She is here to alert me to cultivate the same relationship with myself that I have with her. I now know what love feels like.

Chapter 4

Longing for Meaning: Themes from the Four-Borderline Journey

The Story of S

When I met S, she showed up like an all-American girl—fresh-faced and sun-kissed. She explained how the guy she liked had pulled back, leaving her confused and feeling bad about herself. At this moment, her big smile withered into collapse as the tears poured down her face. She mumbled some words like, "No one will ever love me, and I will be alone forever." The quick shift caught me off guard, and I felt the impact of her deep sadness.

"I really understand . . . I really do," I said.

She looked at me through her tears with a recognition that I knew both as a clinician and as a human. "I know you do," she replied.

And yet, as is the case with most of these clients, I guessed that she would soon find a reason to abandon our connection—a preventative measure so that I would not abandon her first. It is also the common outcome when negative feelings, behavior, and shame become so damaging that the relationship feels beyond repair.

When the pandemic hit, she was called home to quarantine with her family. I wondered how we could do our work when the very people who contributed to her struggle would be locked in a house together. It did not take long for everyone to quickly step into their roles in the toxic dance and for the shit to hit the fan—S feeling homicidal rage and everyone else taking their part, keeping the dynamic alive. The happenings included a fistfight with her dad and brother, the cops trying to talk her down, a serious contemplation of suicide, and S blasting a song called "I Want to Kill All of You" through the house.

During our next few calls, she told me she did not trust me like she did not trust them. At the next session, she said she was a monster. "You feel like a monster," I replied. She hated herself while I tried to help her see that everyone had played a part, including the Prozac she had stopped taking. After S gave me permission to talk to her worn-out parents, I heard their version of how things had been. In closing I said to them, "Just love her. Let her settle back into herself and just let her be."

At our next session, I was fearful that I may have become the enemy again, but sure enough she was there and ready to continue our therapy. We both gazed at each other with acceptance and she let out a smile that said, *I cannot believe all that happened*—all that drama with her family, the police, the aggression. She spoke of it almost as if it had been a bad dream, which can be common when Four-Borderline types get caught in strong emotion. And I returned the smile and could see that she was back to her more grounded self.

What had been healing enough that she could return to her true self for the time being? From my perspective, it was helping her parents see their role and recognize their daughter's cry for help, never giving up on her, really seeing all of her, and coming back together to weave the painful events into an even deeper connection with a little more of her own self-love. And I knew it would happen again and that I would be there—again and again and again—until the message got through that she was lovable and could love herself.

Patterns of Intensity

I have worked with more than one hundred Enneagram type Fours as individual clients or as part of a couple. I have worked with roughly thirty clients with an official Borderline Personality Disorder diagnosis. Some of my closest friends, family members, and students are this personality type. And as one myself, I have had an intimate experience of the motivations, behaviors, and longings of this point of view. When I take the widest, broadest view of the unified pattern I see emerging from the Four-Borderline type, what I see is *longing*—a deep-seated, almost painful, sense of longing.

The German word that Freud and others used to describe longing was *Sehnsucht*, a noun translated into English as "longing," "pining," "yearning," or "craving." "Some psy-chologists use the word *Sehnsucht* to represent thoughts and feelings about all facets of life that are unfinished or imperfect, paired with a yearning for ideal alternative experiences" (Wikipedia, 2023).

This chapter will tell the story of this particular type of Four-Borderline longing and the many characteristics and symptoms of this personality structure that I believe are related to it. I include numerous accounts from my therapy practice, snippets of interviews I conducted with five individuals to dive further into and capture the texture of this longing, images from the many stories I have heard over the years, and some of my own experiences.

The main theme I see in the Four-Borderline is a sense of **being both too much and not enough.** This feeling includes thoughts of not belonging, a feeling of defectiveness, like something is missing or is deeply wrong. This story of being fundamentally broken or not accurately calibrated to this world seems to be almost universally the case for the Four-Borderline types I have spoken with. "There are human emotional notes and chords and we do not know how to synchronize with the music," said one person. One man said he was "hardwired this way." Another woman expressed that, right from the womb, "There was something wrong." Another said they were, "Struggling to feel not defective." And finally, another said, "I will have *too much* written on my grave."

As you can imagine, feeling that one is both too much and not enough plays out strongly in childhood and is sourced there. Many Four-Borderline types found childhood to be filled with strict rules and dogma, creating a split sense of self and a rejection of the joy and freedom once there. A client recently expressed anger in a session about not fully expressing herself in life and pretending to be the good little girl and then, later in life, the good professional woman. She realized she was still holding back who she was at the risk of creating waves or being perceived as difficult. Our therapy involved meeting those deep feelings of grief from a lifetime of pretending. My loving presence served as a proxy until she could be her own loving witness as we met the feelings. As we explored the ways in which she was shutting down or people pleasing, we relaxed the defenses and allowed more acceptance for the life force energy to flow.

This theme of being too much and not enough naturally leads to the second theme: **lacking stability, a sense of self, or a sense of belonging.** Many of us Four-Borderline types never formed a solid sense of self. "I know I am an alien," one woman remarked. Another said her friends "cannot understand my problems." And another said they long "to be complete." When I asked one interviewee what was missing from her life, she said: "a strong sense of self." I then asked what was out of her grasp, to which she replied, "Mainstream acceptance. I have not fit in anywhere." This experience of core disintegration, I believe, is the root cause of the sensitivity this type experiences—the let-downs, dismissal, and the slight reactions hit us right in the core narcissistic wound which is defenseless. (Then comes the rage, further dissociation, etc.)

And, again, it is logical from a place of feeling broken and unstable that there is much compensatory energy spent on **being unique and special.** One interviewee said, "I want to be special and unique ... as just myself." One woman said that her deepest fear was, "Dying without significance in any way to myself and others." This of course is the shadow side of one of the most beautiful things about this type: they are driven to manifest themselves fully through a career or legacy or body of work for the world ... and yet the pain comes when they feel they have no significance if they cannot create a realized or fully expressed version of themselves.

It is important not to miss another theme for this type: the draw towards **creative expression** and **aesthetic beauty**. No doubt due to their sensitivity, Four-Borderlines need creative expression in their day-to-day life and to surround themselves with aesthetically beautiful things. One interviewee spoke of wishing she could summon a Rapunzel tower that was hers, filled with plum velvet, gold curtains, soft fur rugs, a fireplace, and a cat.

Another resounding theme for the Four-Borderline type is **finding their special someone who will fully understand and accept them.** My interviewees describe their desire for a "soul mirroring partner." They speak of this as if, to really be fulfilled in this life, the perfect partner needs to materialize. To be seen and understood by this person would then allow them to feel mirrored and to finally, fully, love themselves. One woman spoke of a romantic style of enmeshment in which "your betterment means mine also, your distance my distance, your love for me is my love for me." A longing for this elusive, romantic partner was prominently at the center of most of the interviews I conducted, along much fantasizing about this mysterious savior. Freud said that, "Love in the form of longing and deprivation lowers the self regard." This strikes me as an incredibly alive truth in the life of the Four-Borderline type.

Looking for love from another to get your own love is dangerous, and I spent much of my life in that pursuit. A striking mirror for this pattern in myself was shown to me when I interviewed my gorgeous, sensitive, and whip-smart niece for this book. Talking to her, I was struck by her level of consciousness and wisdom at just age twenty. What was illuminated to me through her experience is that she does not like anyone ... until she does, and then she cannot stop obsessing, analyzing, and longing. At twenty, she worries about not finding a life partner and even friends with whom she can fully connect—that this is what plagues a beautiful woman at her age makes me sad, but I certainly relate. At times still, below all my confidence and acceptance and growth, there is still a little lingering belief that there will not be someone for me. That I will need to settle for someone I am not attracted to. That someone who is handsome, soulful, smart, passionate, successful, athletic, etc., is reserved for someone else. This is the longing of the Four-Borderline type.

A behavior that this type falls into in order to discern whether or not a potential partner or partner is this longed-for savior—whether they are that special someone who will fully understand and accept them—is **testing**. This testing can be both conscious and unconscious. *Do you like me now? Do you see me now? Do you accept me now? What about when I do or say this?!*

Paired with this urge to test is a paradoxical **fear of abandonment or being misunderstood**. "I feel abandoned so quickly," one interviewee said. Another remembers a pre-verbal feeling of *do not leave me*. One spoke of a sense of there being a "thick barrier" between her and others. And a sort of "magnetic field" that sucks people in and pushes them out at the same time. As if she can neither let them stay or let them go. One woman remarked, "I know I am an alien," and another said her friends cannot understand her problems. Another said, "I am on the outside of the mainstream looking in." Ultimately, the emotional instability, the testing, can keep them more isolated and deepen even more the feeling that no one will ever understand or, even if they do understand, no one will ever stay.

I have also inquired about myself and with clients about the need for **self-protection** for this type—to honor and preserve any sense of self we do have. To not give it away to gain acceptance from others. This can even look like the Four-Borderline type is taking everything—even the critiques, shadows, and aggression of others—for the sake of maintaining connection and love. We are a sponge to it all. So self-protection is something we must cultivate to even stand a chance at a loving sense of self. Indeed, when I asked interviewees what quality would make their life more complete, most said the skill of self-protection—though many said they were not sure how to bring it into their day-to-day life.

Given all of the themes discussed, one longing and need for this type—that perhaps can be seen as the summarizing theme—is the deep tension for this type between **longing for equanimity or stability vs. a constant sense of emotional instability.** Phrases like *embodying self, knowing self,* and *trusting self* are often aspirations for this type. One interviewee described it as longing for a "quietness of the mind." Another person said she longed "to be present where I am would mean I can fully be myself and not be analyzing or deliberating." One person put it: "Stop barking up the wrong tree, and *be* the tree." If you live in a subjective world, you are at the whim of everything and everyone—including your own moods. And this type, as we have discussed, struggles with looking "out there" to try to fill the void or painful inner lack. One interviewee said that she longs for "the version of me that is super powerful and unshakeable, deep but also strong. I now feel deep, but weak—not as resilient as I would like to be." When I speak with this type, when I look at myself, it is revealed that our emotions can be unpredictable or unstable and get in the way of leading a happy and stable life. The deepest longing of all could be said perhaps, to be the longing to be located in oneself, with that self having clear boundaries around it, clear avenues for expression, and a free give and take of love and belonging. The medicine for this type is often embodiment, as connecting with themselves in physical form can often provide the grounded sense they are missing. As a client once said after months of working together: "Before, I was out there far from my body, and now I am right here." They rested their hand on their belly. "I am right here—located in my body."

Facing the Intensity

If the last section did not get this across to you already ... this type can be *a lot*. As painful as it is, I want to share my clinical story of the client who brought me to a decision about not working with more extreme and critical cases of Borderline characteristics any more. Hopefully you can receive this as validation for the struggles you might be having with loving or treating or caring for this type—or for navigating it in yourself.

I felt deep affection for this client, who had an earnest expression of wanting to grow to have a loving relationship and fulfilling career. But mostly what was wanted was just some relief from constantly feeling like they were on a roller coaster of emotion. The swings would come from perceived rejection from a partner, or a meal not going a particular way, or their boss giving constructive feedback. We worked tirelessly, week after week, exploring the ways the client could get a little more sense of self stability, while also enjoying a relationship and a career. We continuously went over the suicide protocol along with the self-soothing measures whenever they felt a sense of emptiness or impulse as the emotional swings were sometimes too much to bear for the client at times.

I remember lying awake many nights after a message was left saying something like, "Tamra, I do not want to live anymore and tonight is the night." Welfare checks, police, and hospital visits were the norm for our work together. Just when things were starting to get better and the client enjoyed a sense of accomplishment and celebration, there would be another dramatic happening.

Unfortunately, I had to stop working with the client when I received a death threat from one of their parents who was also in and out of psychological crisis, as well as a separate threat to sue me from their other parent, and a grievance by their spouse. I will always miss this client and send positive, heartfelt feelings their way. I am unable to divulge more of the reasons and events surrounding this particular client, but this story illustrates that working with the extreme versions of this type of personality can be hard and even scary work for all involved.

And, hardships aside, the experience of sitting with Four-Borderline types, for me, is being in the presence of an openness and authenticity that I do not experience with most people. I can feel their earnest search for the truth and the pureness of their hearts. When I interviewed the interviewees, the actual experience of these meetings made me feel vibrant, impacted, protective, and nurturing. I could feel the depth, longing, and beauty in each of them.

The short snippets below as this chapter comes to a close is to give you a glimpse into the nature of Borderline characteristics that may surface when a client is more activated by their deeper wound. Below are some impressions, a collage of moments and images, to take in in order to help you feel the experience from the inside out. Perhaps it reflects your own experience or reminds you of someone you love.

A new client came in bright and wide-eyed and then collapsed into tears. As he tried explaining, he looked at me through his tears, he recognized that I knew both as a clinician and as a human what he was going through. "I know you do," he said. "You have the right to be sad," I said, "I am here."

A woman is standing knee-deep in a fountain shouting, "You just do not understand me!" Her boyfriend stands below, shoulders collapsed, embarrassed, wondering how long this episode will last. How many more times can I try to make her feel understood? *He wonders.*

He texts his girlfriend, I went too deep this time, *as blood drips from the sink down to the floor. The only thing he can feel is the terror of what if she never texts back? What if I've ruined things forever?*

She is outraged and hurt that her ex canceled last-minute. Her thoughts go like this: How could they do this to me? I am so generous, and they are so mean. They know how much effort and care I put into planning the evening and they had the nerve to tell me they were "being brave." I hate their family and where they lived and they never gave me what I wanted, but I cannot stop thinking about them and wondering why they did this to me. I just wanted a nice evening so they could see how good I look and that I can handle everything that happened. All my friends tell me how wonderful I am and how controlling and arrogant they were. Why can't I just get over them and move on? I do not like being rejected by someone I don't even like in the first place.

She doesn't trust him, but she cannot leave. Her thoughts go like this: I never leave. I wish I could. They got into it again last night. He was drinking and she brought up him talking to his old girlfriend. He started yelling, saying she was crazy and needed to get a life. She was shaking mad. But she didn't argue back since he just might leave this time. She kept her feelings to herself and tried to get through another night—not knowing if he would still be there in the morning. But her mind is spinning. I feel like I am talking to a moron—he definitely doesn't get me at all. But I am afraid he will leave me, so I don't want to do therapy with him. I feel like my nervous system is on overdrive. I cannot eat or sleep. I am so exhausted.

My current relationship is so amazing. I am having so much fun, yet I am so scared since no one has ever really understood and seen me before. I am not sure I want to be with him, yet it feels so good. I am still so hurt by my ex. I cannot believe I tolerated his avoidance. I thought it was all my fault. I do not want him in my life. He just does not get how hurtful he is. It was a blessing we broke up. I am finally feeling happy. I really should not have any communication with him; the last time I received a text I cried the entire day at work. I don't even know why I miss him.

Chapter 5

Healing the Four-Borderline Type

This chapter contains the healing tools and modalities I have seen work for myself, my clients, and my Four-Borderline's loved ones. Before you read more about the tools below, remember that, if you identify as this type, you may react to these tools as being too mundane, too everyday, too boring. Yes. That is their medicine. If you employ them with self-love and consistency, you will benefit from them.

Healing Tools

Practice **self-love** every day. You may think this means baths and pedicures. Those are great, if you love them, but I mean something far deeper than that. Self-love means, first and foremost, knowing that you are a lovable and worthy person. You are not flawed or broken. Try saying that in the mirror a good ten times a day. As you do, look into your own eyes to register the message deeply. It is also good exercise to invite others to share your good qualities with you. Try to receive and breathe in the yumminess of what they share. Feel free to direct them in what to share as well—ask them to remind you of the things you are trying to remind yourself.

If you can, try to find **lightness and humor** in your days. Try experiencing yourself with care and ease. When you wake in the morning, smile and summon a feeling of "all is well"—at least for a moment.

And at some point before you start your day, try **meditation**. If your mind is chewing on too much to sit still, then use a meditation app to guide you through a visualization. The goal is to start to become curious and friendly to your own experience. If you do not have coffee grinds in your fridge, shrug your shoulders and say, "That is okay. I am doing my best. Guess it is the overpriced cafe once again."

I recommend a meditation called the Golden Triangle. Here is how to do it. Sit in a comfortable position with your butt firmly placed. Take a few moments and let your mind have all the thoughts it wants and your body have all the movements it wants. Stay in this place for a good five minutes. My professor called this "letting the dogs out." Then settle into your seat and really feel your butt against the surface. Feel every inch of you there. Do a deep inhale and pull energy down into your bottom and then extend out through your bottom the image of big tree trunks that root deep into the universe. Really feel into your roots and envision them going deep into the universe. Stay with this for about ten minutes as you really begin to feel a sense of being grounded. Once you feel anchored, now visualize pulling a golden light down from the sky and into your being, starting with the top of your head. Fill every inch of your being with this golden light—do not miss any part of you. No need to rush. Once golden light fills your entire body and being, revisit your roots that extend deep into the universe. Spend a little time experiencing yourself as now both full and stable.

Nutrition for your mental health is vital and is increasingly part of the conversation. Really pay attention to what you eat and if you need help register for an online course or go to a professional to get guidance. Food can really alter our brain chemistry, so it is something to be taken seriously.

Exercise daily, if you possibly can. We need to move the feelings and anxiety through the body. If not, they will stagnate. Every Four-Borderline needs consistent movement practice to get in the body, out of the head, and to move through the feelings. And when we move, we encounter new experiences including people, places, and things. There are so many types of movement exercises—walking, dance, jogging, yoga, and all the popular movement meditations. And movement has a magical way of helping us not to hold all the big feelings within ourselves but to let them out to be held in a bigger way by the universe, God, or whatever you believe can hold and support you.

Spend time in **nature**. Nature is perfection and beauty. As I was listening to a panel of Enneagram Fours led by Beatrice Chestnut, I was surprised by the amount of time the participants talked about gardening, relationships, and movement. A few of them talked specifically about the way they feel in nature, expressing that nature was a perfect embodiment of the natural perfection of things, while also being able to hold their intense and overwhelming emotions. In hypothesizing about the significance of nature, it seems that most Four-Borderlines are not grounded; nature can bring them grounding.

Creativity is so important. All the energy that is you is best expressed so it does not stay bottled up inside. Say, move, write what is happening on the inside. If you can, try to add something creative to your daily routine. And then share your creations with your friends or family or the world, if you like. You inspire others.

Create **structure** in life. There is a tendency for this type to follow their mood in almost everything, so a daily routine is key for maintaining stability. As the Enneagram Institute states (www.enneagraminstitute.com/type-4), "A wholesome self-discipline takes many forms, from sleeping regular hours to working regularly to exercising regularly, and has a cumulative, strengthening effect. Since it comes from yourself, a healthy self-discipline is not contrary to your freedom or individuality." Your routine should still include time for daydreaming, creative projects, dancing, and just roaming. A well-rounded structure serves body, mind, heart, and spirit/soul. For example, a yoga class, an academic class or something that feeds your mind, some contemplative reading, social time, and praying before sleep. Whatever the activities are, they should serve to balance all of the realms of self.

Consider using **psychedelics** in a therapeutic, safe, and contained environment and with an experienced guide. See more about my experience with this in the next chapter.

Another big thing for such sensitive and open types is **boundaries**. When someone has wronged the Four-Borderline, or they just do not feel good around another, they must learn to draw a boundary. This can look like taking space or letting a person know that you are not okay with a certain behavior. You can still like who they are at their core and still hold hope for them, but you can say no.

Being okay with losing someone or even purposely letting someone go. Life is about renewal; not everyone can come on our journey with us. The experience of losing someone can help us have the stability and confidence to enter new relationships without the anxiety and dread of the loss—you know you can survive it. Be careful of the idealization of who the person was to you or the nostalgia that you will never feel the same with someone new. You will, I promise. It just takes an entire new set of neural pathways and a thicker skin.

If there is one variable that I have seen over the years that will promote deeper healing and integration, it is **taking time to be single**. I find with many of my clients that if they stay single long enough, they are able to build a solid sense of self and maintain and tolerate all the emotional ups and downs in their life.

But **watch out for isolation**. I had a client recently say that she felt like she was not getting her needs met by her parents and friends and did not want to burden her boyfriend. Her cure for it was to withdraw. There is such a deep sensitivity to being rejected or not understood that it is easier to just hibernate alone. And since there is usually a feeling of not belonging in groups, it is just easy to tell yourself that you are different or too unique to have friends. However, this story is false and completely removes you from the possibility of connection, attunement, and love.

Of course the **Enneagram** is another wonderful tool to use on this journey. There are three aspects I want to point out here about this powerful tool.

The first is to use the tool of the **developmental stages** within your Enneagram type, as we discussed and laid out in Chapter 2. In considering the levels of development, this is a wonderful tool with which to track your evolution. And remember our evolution is not exact—you will know if you are experiencing more peace and joy in a consistent fashion. And your friends and family and co-workers will also most likely be able to reflect this back to you. You will know you are leveling up the more you can identify more with your deepest Self and less with your sense of self. The experience is a calmer and more peaceful experience with less response to the external world as a trigger of any conditioning. The Four at the higher levels is more rooted in their heart and their attention is more on others and less on themselves. In the Enneagram, this is called the *missing piece*: when this deeper quality is met, the experience of the individual changes.

Another way to use the Enneagram as a growth tool is by deepening your **awareness of the three centers: head, heart and body**. When these centers are aligned, we enjoy more balance.

And finally a third Enneagram tool: **instincts and/or subtypes**. The instincts, as I will refer to them, are various categories our personality pays attention to stay safe. There are three main instinctual types: self-preservation, social, and sexual (also called one-to-one). For the self-presentation type, their attention is on well-being, finances, money, and the overall state of the self. The social instinct is focused on others and community and going outside self as a way to engage and feel belonging. The sexual instinct is about passion, drive, and transmitting energy through yourself, and potentially an intimate other. We all have these evolutionary drives and we seem to default to one or two with the third left in our blind spot, a little more out of our awareness. As an example, before I moved to Boulder, I was very much in my sexual and self-preservation subtype. Once I settled in, got my dog Bella, joined a number of groups, and made new friends, I became much more a part of the social instinct.

When we balance across all three instincts, we balance all three centers, and we keep our attention on where we are developmentally. We can enjoy greater well-being as a fully expressed human.

Presence and Validation in Therapy

When a loved one or therapist mirrors and validates the emotional experience of the Four-Borderline, it serves as a proxy to build and integrate a sense of self for the type as they learn to build and feel their own sense of self.

Healers and family members: know that the best way to be with a Four-Borderline type is to validate their feelings and attune to them. Ask them to go deeper, to say more, to let them know you really *want to understand*. Even when they are sharing anger or sadness, ask them to tell you more. Sometimes just being *asked* is a corrective experience; it has a way of settling the nervous system and rewiring the brain. This kind of curiosity might be a way of relating that many Four-Borderlines have not experienced a lot. (If they had, they probably would not be how they are!)

If the younger Four-Borderline did not receive attuned validation from a parent, then, as we have discussed already, a sense of self never fully formed in their center. They then developed an over reliance on the outside world for validation and overdeveloped the habit of *thinking* their feelings—rather than feeling them. Fueled by a lot of thought activity, these feelings become overwhelming and exaggerated. In Object

Relations terms, such a fragmented self is not solid or separate enough to be fully experienced without taking in others or another experience. There is such an expansive, boundaryless quality to the self that it gets confused with others in a way that makes one question who they are and what is expected. And the ability to self-regulate has not developed, so an auto-regulation (withdrawal) or a co-regulation (dependence) may happen. In summary, it is incredibly destabilizing.

But the helper is wise to remember that holding space for a Four-Borderline includes the ability to set the boundaries in the relationship while also maintaining a balanced inner experience. The inner experience would ideally include a relaxed nervous system and lack of fear in engaging with the person who may be intense, anxious, and sometimes aggressive. It is also beneficial to work through a lot of counter-transference that may come up before sitting with someone who is this sensitive. One example of what might come up for the supporter is finding the person too needy and intrusive. If you are a therapist, you might need to make sure you can tolerate their anger and criticism of you as the therapist. Four-Borderlines need us to accept and validate their exaggerated emotions while also setting firm boundaries so that they feel safe and that they do not have to protect others from their own intensity.

As a therapist, my approach with such clients is that everything is allowed and everything is reflected until the client can hold their experience themselves—which could take many years. There is no benefit for the client to feel ashamed for inhabiting their bad self while they cannot experience their lack of self or their good self. It is best to hold this for them until they can experience emotional equanimity. Week after week, the client will hopefully report a more positive experience in their day-to-day life. Their nervous system has to adjust to this newly found peace so that the old patterns are not continuously recreated. And the client's story, while so important, needs to be carefully examined so the beliefs and behaviors that do not serve can be challenged.

I recently had a therapy session with a new therapist for myself and my experience was profound. As I was swirling around about the beginning of a new semester and if I would ever find a life partner, I had an experience of being witnessed and joined so directly that, in that moment, I found myself. I found myself! I was right there, with no need to swirl or ruminate. What an incredible relief. My shoulders softened, my heart opened, and my belly felt full.

Ultimately of course, suffering Four-Borderlines must slowly learn to sit with ourselves, feel into our hurt, grief, and become *our own* presence and nurturing. From this space, external invalidation and dismissal will become far less triggering.

In my work, I notice that being a Four-Borderline myself while treating Four-Borderline clients can be exponentially helpful. Because I personally know the terrain of the fixations and patterns, I can navigate the client's path with much more precision and give mirroring and attunement in the places that are most in need of healing. With most of these clients, it is as if I have a direct experience of their experience, which they find relieving as it is the opposite of feeling missed and dismissed.

Healing Relationships

Most Four personalities have an anxious-avoidant attachment style, so we tend to attract avoidant styles until we are more secure. It is best if you can choose to partner with someone secure so that if you are completely yourself, the person will not be as reactive to you. If you can also choose someone who is higher in the level of development, according to the Enneagram, then there is also less likelihood that someone will react from their own unmet wounding. A good rule of thumb is to see if someone can respond versus react and this usually indicates their psycho-spiritual integration.

Because there is a certain level of intensity of this type and an interest in relating, it is probably best to pick a less rational type and a more dynamic type as a partner—someone who is super passionate with bigger feelings and also wants a deep intimate relationship would be a resonant choice. Someone who is more rigid and who is more worried about security may not be a wise choice. It is worth mentioning that each of us has the capacity to be all of the energies while also not being fixated in a particular lens, so the healthier the better. The healthier you are, the healthier type of a partner you will attract.

In looking at the Enneagram statistics regarding the majority of relationships for type Fours, a Four and a Nine are most commonly partnered. There are also some in the Enneagram community who say that the healthiest partnership is a Four and an Eight, since both are intense beings. The Eight is more outwardly expressed and the Four expresses their creativity outwardly. Both can be strong and assertive and like the beauty and experience of leading life to the fullest.

Within the Enneagram model, if the Four personalities are feeling stressed, they will head toward Two-type behavior, which looks like it's more caretaking and possessive. They will not be satisfied with a partner that is aloof or who does not enjoy affection or spending a lot of time together. The point again being that well-being with yourself is everything in a relationship for a Four-Borderline type.

Within relationships, Four-Borderlines must remain aware of their own feelings. There are many times I have feelings when I am not fully in integrity with myself. I may say yes when I mean no, overextend myself, or not have the conversation I need to have in order to stay in alignment with myself and in right-relationship with others. It is helpful if you are able to speak openly and authentically to people around you about your experience. It is also necessary to create rituals so that you manage feelings daily without letting them build and overwhelm the system. It is no wonder that "equanimity" is the ultimate goal of this type as emotional balance makes all the difference for us to stay grounded and open in relationships.

I grew up believing what I did and the feedback I received was an indication of *who I was*. I gathered feedback through experiences of how popular, kind, athletic, pretty, smart, etc., I was. If a popular boy liked me, that meant I was popular. When I made homecoming court, that meant I was liked.

Throughout the years, love and work remained the same toxic sources of my own sense of self. It was not until I started questioning who I was that everything started to be seen differently. Finally, I had the experience while living at the ashram that told me that me *without any criteria* has always been me.

To this day, I still need to be careful not to chase the latest guy, or business, or workout, and to deeply remember and experience that I have the experience of me no matter what happens in the external world. If I am rejected, that does not need to define who I am.

Group Work

Some say one needs individual therapy first in order to be prepared for group therapy. Group therapy is more of the process kind, it is a "free for all." The facilitator uses group theory, including bridging and other techniques, to help foster healing for each of the group members. Such groups inevitably start to replicate the family of origin and participants start to project members onto the group, finding upsetting reminders of parents and/or siblings. Group members are usually invited to notice that the overall way they navigate the family life will be most likely similar to how they navigate the group dynamics.

Breakthroughs and realizations can only happen when participants put their thoughts and feelings into words so that the facilitator and other members can help them through the experience. This can reveal for the participant how they are, in a way, "teaching" others to treat them. The group may also unearth the participants' judgments and beliefs about others and the world and how they feel they must show up in a group setting. If a Four-Borderline type has a good therapist and a somewhat stable sense of self, then a group is a wonderful tool to add to your healing regime.

A word of caution about groups for the Four-Borderline: interview the facilitator and other members of the group so that you are not unintentionally wounded by something you may not be ready for or by unconscious material the group may be playing along with the facilitator. I have seen disasters where there is a full collapse from the Four-Borderline once confronted in the group setting. I have seen rage come out from Four-Borderlines in group settings. And I have also witnessed success and powerful healing, including for myself, in a well-guided group.

Self-Healing

A client of mine was struggling with a conflict in themselves. They were being very self-abusing, while also getting confused about who they were in the world and feeling unsafe in being their biggest self.

We explored how there is a lot of safety in being small and staying safe. There were many childhood memories about being too much, too big, or too *anything*. Any thought and belief that opposed the idea of who they thought they should be became an attack on self. In exploring, we found a way to resource a really good feeling from childhood to help embody this feeling within their experience.

For me, the only way to help a client step away from self-abuse is to give them an experience of their own deepest Self that does not change. This self-embodiment can be a way to work towards a fuller feeling of Self so as not to get caught in the ego, which is always changing and is thus fundamentally fragile and unstable. Then hopefully the client has a "saving grace" to access when life starts to feel overwhelming, and they lose the sense of themselves.

Week after week, I invite clients to shift from their insecure, confused, and exhausted ways to a place of secure, trusting, and vibrant presence. It is not easy—but it is simple: we need to keep coming back to our Self, as it is never-ending, equanimous, and present. This is how a Four-Borderline type heals.

Chapter 6

Intensity Is Power

In pondering my own life journey and the beautiful individuals I have worked with and know, it is tough to point to exactly what will work to help a Four-Borderline heal; many things help, but there is no prescription.

It is easy to pathologize this type because society pathologizes it. We see this in the way artists are often called "crazy"; the way women are dismissed as "hormonal" and "too much"; the way jilted lovers are labeled "clingy."

But I am here to say: Dear Four-Borderline type, you are just as capable of healing as anyone else on this confusing, wild planet. And now, as this book comes to a close, I want to share that there is even healing beyond the personal and psychological, beyond the traditional tools and therapeutic approach. Please do those things first, but I want to plan a seed of some other existential and even mystical options that you may find useful.

Marianne Williamson recently launched a new series, *Miraculous Love*, which I was watching the other day as I poured myself into scrolling through Match.com. As I lost myself in swiping through the faces of these mysterious men, a wave of dark, hopeless, despairing thinking arose in me. *How am I going to find my person? Will there be someone for me?*

Then Marianne's words reached me, reminding me that *we are already complete*. The illusion is that we need to be more or different than we are right now to be okay. To be enough. It is the thinking mind and the contracted body that creates the experience of being separate and fearful. As Dr. Gabor Mate says, "Trauma is a separation of self." What if, right now, we could believe and feel that we are absolutely okay? Marianne Williamson was saying that we *are* love. Right now. I might offer instead the words: complete, perfect, and enough. So, in that moment, I asked God: *Please, let me surrender to what keeps me from believing all is well. Please let me see the truth of who I am and who we all are. Please let me see life as a damn miracle.*

Now, I am perhaps no further along in my own reality with finding a partner, however I have trust and a sense of peace that it will happen. I leaned on the wisdom and presence of another — Marianne Williamson in this case — to ground myself, remind myself of my truth, and come back to a place of stability.

When in doubt, I encourage the Four-Borderline type to return, again and again, to a relationship with a loving and accepting therapist and or capable friend. It is through this mirroring and hand-holding that an individual can explore, discover, and feel the deepest depth of themselves. This includes bringing forth all that is hidden to be with someone as you experience the anger, sadness, confusion, and ultimately joy of all the traumas of life.

We all need help and support as we integrate all parts of ourselves — the good and the bad, the wounded and the brave — so that we can finally experience something inside ourselves that is beyond even what is good and what is bad. As we heal, our experience of Self can grow, until one day the events of life are like passing waves that do not cause turbulence. As a client said to me once, "I do not want to be a Velcro dart board, I want to be a silk one" — where nothing sticks, it just slides off.

The Enneagram also holds the teaching of transcending one's type and embracing the totality and wisdom of all the types. We can do this on a personality level as we work on embodying all of the virtues of the nine Enneagram points — serenity, humility, veracity, equanimity, non-attachment, courage, sobriety, innocence, and action. (See: www2.cruzio. com/~zdino/psychology/enneagram.maitri.htm). But we can also do this by incorporating all the deeper Holy Ideas that A. H. Almaas points to that live on the spiritual level. (See: www.

diamondapproach.org/glossary/refinery_phrases/enneagram-holy-ideas).

As it so wisely says to the Four in *The Wisdom of the Enneagram*, "Avoid lengthy conversations in your imagination, particularly if they are negative, resentful, or even excessively romantic. These conversations are essentially unreal and at best only rehearsals for action—although, as you know, you almost never say or do what you imagine you will. Instead of spending time imagining your life and relationships, begin to live them" (Russ Hudson, The Enneagram Institute). Yes, again and again and again, I see the medicinal power of relationships for the Four-Borderline type. Typically, I see couples with pretty opposite personalities pairing up. Their deepest life lessons are unearthed by these dynamic differences. Partnership—such a challenging experience when you have children, in-laws, financial and health concerns, etc.—is rich ground indeed.

Another way to grow is to have trusted friends show you what you may not be able to see yet. What if these trusted friends were part of a community that met weekly so that together you could be mirrored by multiple points of view? The group I created with Ori Zimmels as our teacher is one of my most precious weekly rituals. Week after week, Ori pours his wisdom into us so that we may have an easier time in life. (Thank you, Ori, for helping us rest in the center of self.)

Psychedelics

I am very excited by the prospects of legal psychedelics. It seems that MDMA is the miracle drug for the type of complex PTSD exhibited by so many of us. When paired with Psilocybin, it seems to offer an embodied, transpersonal effect.

Legal, supported psychedelic experiences have been a game-changer for many Four-Borderline people I know—including myself. I have had several clients who did the work with guides and then worked with me for integration. I saw them go from dissociation to embodiment so rapidly it shocked me, and I have even completed therapy with a number of them.

Before my own psychedelic experience, I had studied and been around so much spiritual language I could really "talk the talk"; and yet until I did the drugs, I had absolutely no *lived experience* of the concept of oneness that I was speaking of.

Many of my friends in Boulder do psychedelics as a path to healing. I was always scared about altering my experience and heard myself more than once say that I wanted the "pure way." Well, the "pure way" was never quite reaching the inner psychological wound of my infant surgery that I longed to heal. My intuition was telling me that all my relationship patterns and pain were pointing directly back to my month in the hospital after I was born. So with a little doubt and a lot of excitement, I headed into a weekend with a psychedelic guide.

The main point with this type of medicine is that setting, pre- and post-integration sessions, along with the companionships of an experienced guide make the party drug instead a deep, and dare I say life-changing, experience. I did the recommended dose for my weight of MDMA. The setting was gorgeous and my guide came highly recommended. I allowed myself the entire weekend for the experience to really give the journey full space.

As I have shared in this book, I have always struggled with not being in my body, a feeling of emptiness, and needing to control or leave most relationships—business and romance. So my intentions that weekend were centered around these issues, yet I also wanted to be open as I wanted to welcome whatever experience was necessary for my healing.

Once the medicine took effect after about thirty to sixty minutes, I felt as if I was floating in what felt like an amniotic sac of yummy liquid that flowed through every cell of my body. I remarked out loud that I loved everyone and everything, including myself.

After a little time, a voice in me said I wanted to be held like a little baby. So I asked my guide if she would hold me. She put me in her lap and stroked my head for over an hour. I was able to have the experience of feeling fully loved, being touched, and receiving care. Perfectly, the guide was about to go on break, so I was able to experience the feeling of someone close to me giving me care and then also leaving, but knowing that she would come back. Even though I trusted she would come back, I still found myself opening my eyes and peeking to see if she was back, along with some dialogue within me reminding myself that I would be okay no matter what. And she came back, of course.

I had always thought there was sexual abuse in my past. I wondered if something horrible and forgotten like that would explain so much of my pain. So I asked the question during the journey and then waited for the answer.

What finally came was the insight that being left in a hospital without being able to feel my body may have had the same effect as being molested. As I realized this, I etched into my consciousness that I did not have to carry that story any longer. And that is when the yummy lava-like liquid I was floating in filled my sexual area, and I finally felt lit up after a full lifetime of feeling sexually numb.

Six hours went by pretty quickly and I started to move around a bit. By the end, I was standing and swaying with the music. Then the journey came to a close.

The post-integration experiences brought home a number of things: apparently my belly, where the surgery happened, was contracting for about forty-five minutes during the journey. I had not noticed it, but the guide had.

I also came away knowing that my deepest truth is not in my head but in the very deepest part of myself. I also deeply feel and have experienced that love is the answer to everything.

After the journey, I enjoyed a bliss bubble for a few days. And then, of course, my mind tried to pull me back to my old familiar patterns, which brought up a bit of sadness and melancholy. Such journeys put a lot of serotonins in the system, so you can feel a drop after, while also experiencing and continuing to clear out the pain from a more objective vantage point. But now my focus is less on the story and more on clearing the *actual* hurt and pain.

I am grateful to now have guided psychedelics as part of my healing tools.

Powerfully Intense

Less and less am I interested in my own story. As a matter of fact, I am sick to death of it. So much that it does not have any power over me to lure me back in. What I am more excited by is the day-to-day reality of being with everything. And in our turbulent times, it is a tall order to be with everything. So we do as best we can as we focus on never, ever leaving ourselves.

When did our culture get so cut off from emotions? Why do many of us move through the world like talking heads? When did we forget to inhabit our bodies? Maybe we can blame the Industrial Revolution and the era it introduced of valuing machines, intelligence, and innovation over human life. Maybe we can blame the forty-hour work week. Whatever the reason, many people do not experience sensations or emotions and somehow manage to get through their days utilizing the body as a vehicle for accomplishing work and accomplishing pleasure.

This is the power of the Four-Borderline; our heady, removed culture desperately needs our qualities. Imagine if we all viewed depth, meaning, and beauty as the key to a well-lived life, as the Four-Borderline does. What if we were all sensitive to how we or others were treated, just as the Four-Borderline is. What if poetry and art became the new currency of success and productivity? And what if authenticity was revered as much as identity? It would definitely be a different world indeed.

I like to imagine a time when us Four-Borderlines will not feel like such unicorns. We would flaunt our peacock feathers and not feel shame. We would become everything we desire in life while feeling met and understood. We would dance while everyone was looking.

We can start now, no matter what the external world is doing, by honoring all of our components of experience and not just our mind. We can wonder why we feel sad when our partner barks at us for asking an innocent question. We can feel the butterflies in our stomach when we walk down a dark street. We can allow the visual images and auditory voices whenever they seem to come. We can also give credibility to our intuition when we just *know* something. We can give credit to our full range of thoughts, feelings, and sensation for ourselves and others.

I honor and bow to every soul who has had to endure this walk, this sometimes cursed-seeming journey of being a Four-Borderline type. You have not given up. You picked yourself up from that last messy fall and dusted yourself off with your head held high. We will be together supporting each other with every new variation of lived experience—the heartbreak and the joy.

Please do not ever stop telling the truth. Please do not ever stop searching for the deeper meaning. Please do not ever stop feeling. And please do not ever stop being you. As a matter of fact, become the biggest and boldest you. Become your true self.

Know that the journey of *you* will never stop. The path of you will be a unique and daily ritual. Enjoy swimming in the deepest ocean of you. And life and others will continue to point you towards what you need, so do not worry about knowing. Rest in the unknown.

A Closing Offering: Tamra's Mantra

Look around and within: what can I appreciate right here and right now?

I am the uniqueness of the unique.

I do not trust my story; I trust the deepest me that never changes.

I am enough.

I am so happy to be me.

I can feel the vibrancy of me.

I give and receive without pride.

I ask for help when I cannot see.

I embody my deepest most authentic Self that does not change.

My all-is-well feeling is being myself.

I love everyone and everything, including me.

When someone leaves, I still have me.

When someone is here, I have me and them.

I hug each of my cells.

My gift is to simply be my deepest self without effort.

Appendix

Orientations of the Four-Borderline Type

Core belief/Unconscious childhood message: *It is not okay to be myself, too functional, or too happy*

I would have most liked to hear as a child: *You are seen for who you are*

Basic desire: *"To be myself"* (Eli Jaxon-Bear)

Holy Path/Virtue: *"Equanimity"* (Eli Jaxon-Bear)

Holy Idea: *"Holy Origin"* (A. H. Almaas)

Passion/Sin: *"Envy"* (Eli Jaxon-Bear)

Essence: *"Joy"* (Eli Jaxon-Bear)

Missing Piece: *Holy freedom and humility*

Basic fear: *"Being without identity or personal significance (being unseen)"* (Russ Hudson, The Enneagram Institute)

Fixation: *"Melancholy"* (Eli Jaxon-Bear)

Attention moves to: *Being unique*

I am most often asking myself: *Do they see how special I am?*

Reason for reactions: *I am not special*

Reactions: *Controlling oneself/other*

Core need: *To be seen*

Defense mechanism: *Introjection*

Distortion: *Self-indulgence*

Trap: *"Authenticity"* (Eli Jaxon-Bear)

Avoidance: *"Feeling lost"* (Eli Jaxon-Bear)

Object relations: *Parents were not attuned*

Talking style: *Complaining*

Idealization/You may glorify that you are: *Elite*

Problem patterns: *Making negative comparisons*

Karen Horney/Naranjo: *Moving away/withdrawing (I am smaller than the world)*

Ego/ID/Superego: *Ego withdrawn/Identity focused*
Dichotomy: *"Analytic/Disoriented"* (Eli Jaxon-Bear)
Red flag/Average to unhealthy: *I am ruining my life/wasting my opportunities*
Wake-up call/getting more stressed: *I hold onto/intensify feelings through my imagination*
When stressed out: *Being temperamental; Making others walk on eggshells*
Addictions: *"Over-indulgence in rich foods, sweets, alcohol to alter mood, to socialize, and for emotional consolation. Lack of physical activity. Bulimia. Depression. Tobacco, prescription drugs, or heroin for social anxiety. Cosmetic surgery to erase rejected features."* (Russ Hudson, Enneagram Institute)
Leaden Rule/If I was upset with someone I might be tempted to: *Make them feel like they are insignificant*
Invitation/Higher Purpose: *To be forgiving and to use everything in life for my growth and renewal; Invitation to observe yourself and other without judgment or expectations*
I am good or okay when: *I am true to myself*
Examples of Type Fours: *"Rumi, Frédéric Chopin, Tchaikovsky, Gustav Mahler, Jackie Kennedy Onassis, Edgar Allen Poe, Yukio Mishima, Virginia Woolf, Anne Frank, Karen Blixen/ Isak Dinesen, Anaïs Nin, Tennessee Williams, J.D. Salinger, Anne Rice, Frida Kahlo, Diane Arbus, Martha Graham, Rudolf Nureyev, Cindy Sherman, Hank Williams, Billie Holiday, Judy Garland, Maria Callas, Miles Davis, Keith Jarrett, Joni Mitchell, Bob Dylan, Paul Simon, Leonard Cohen, Cat Stevens, Ferron, Cher, Stevie Nicks, Annie Lennox, Prince, Sarah McLachlan, Alanis Morrisette, Feist, Florence (+ the Machine) Welch, Amy Winehouse, Ingmar Bergman, Lars von Trier, Marlon Brando, Jeremy Irons, Angelina Jolie, Winona Ryder, Kate Winslet, Nicolas Cage, Johnny Depp, Kat Von D., Criss Angel,* Streetcar Named Desire's *Blanche duBois."* (Russ Hudson, The Enneagram Institute)

MANTRA
BOOKS

EASTERN RELIGION & PHILOSOPHY

We publish books on Eastern religions and philosophies. Books
that aim to inform and explore the various traditions that
began in the East and have migrated West.
If you have enjoyed this book, why not tell other readers by
posting a review on your preferred book site.

The Less Dust the More Trust
Participating in The Shamatha Project, Meditation and Science
Adeline van Waning, MD PhD
The inside-story of a woman participating in frontline
meditation research, exploring the interfaces of mind-practice,
science and psychology.
Paperback: 978-1-78099-948-7 ebook: 978-1-78279-657-2

I Know How To Live, I Know How To Die
The Teachings of Dadi Janki: A warm, radical, and life-
affirming view of who we are, where we come from, and what
time is calling us to do
Neville Hodgkinson
Life and death are explored in the context of frontier science
and deep soul awareness.
Paperback: 978-1-78535-013-9 ebook: 978-1-78535-014-6

Living Jainism
An Ethical Science
Aidan Rankin, Kanti V. Mardia
A radical new perspective on science rooted in intuitive
awareness and deductive reasoning.
Paperback: 978-1-78099-912-8 ebook: 978-1-78099-911-1

Ordinary Women, Extraordinary Wisdom
The Feminine Face of Awakening
Rita Marie Robinson
A collection of intimate conversations with female spiritual
teachers who live like ordinary women, but are engaged
with their true natures.
Paperback: 978-1-84694-068-2 ebook: 978-1-78099-908-1

The Way of Nothing
Nothing in the Way
Paramananda Ishaya
A fresh and light-hearted exploration of the amazing reality of
nothingness.
Paperback: 978-1-78279-307-6 ebook: 978-1-78099-840-4

Readers of ebooks can buy or view any of these bestsellers by
clicking on the live link in the title. Most titles are published
in paperback and as an ebook. Paperbacks are available in
traditional bookshops. Both print and ebook formats are
available online.

Find more titles and sign up to our readers' newsletter at
http://www.johnhuntpublishing.com/mind-body-spirit. Follow
us on Facebook at https://www.facebook.com/OBooks and
Twitter at https://twitter.com/obooks.